Alvah Lillie Frisbie

**Songs of Sorrow and Micellaneous Poems**

Alvah Lillie Frisbie

**Songs of Sorrow and Micellaneous Poems**

ISBN/EAN: 9783744709897

Printed in Europe, USA, Canada, Australia, Japan

Cover: Foto ©Thomas Meinert / pixelio.de

More available books at **www.hansebooks.com**

# SONGS OF SORROW.

# SONGS OF SORROW

AND

## MISCELLANEOUS POEMS,

BY

## REV. A. L. FRISBIE.

DES MOINES:
MILLS & COMPANY
1873.

DES MOINES:

MILLS & COMPANY, PRINTERS.

DEDICATED

TO

# MY ANGEL WIFE.

"Volo ut ubi sum, et illi sint mecum."

762873

# SONGS OF SORROW.

### *DARKNESS AND SILENCE.*

Into the gladness of our happy dwelling
  Came first a fear and then a grievous pain;
Came first sad prophecy, then sad fulfilling,
  As love's blent life was rudely rent in twain;

And she who was the very soul and center
  Of home and hope through sweet and sunlit years,
Before us passed the shadowed door to enter,—
  The unknown life of unseen higher spheres.

She passed before us and our eyes were holden;
  An utter darkness fell upon our sight;
What light she saw, what forms, what gate-way golden,
  We knew not, saw not in our heavy night.

And still that sea of darkness rolls behind her;
  Still veils and hides the place of her abode;
No patient, prayerful, tearful quest can find her;
  She has become a mystery of God.

Into a silence awful and confounding,
  Deep as the stillness with which night comes down,
Dumb as the Sphinx her problem still propounding,
  Death swept away our loved and loving one.

O could this cruel silence but be broken,—
  The cloud dispelled that shuts her from our sight,—
O could she give of present love some token,—
  How would our hearts stand still with strange delight.

O could she give some sign to our inquiring,—
  Shine in a star-beam, whisper in a breeze;
How would it soothe us in our long desiring
  If only we might say, "She knows and sees!"

Could she but speak from out the heavenly places,
  Could she but say, "I live and think of you,—
In glory e'en I miss your dear embraces,—
  I'll give you welcome when your journey's through;

## DARKNESS AND SILENCE.

How would our souls rise up with glad assurance
　　Of what we must believe through joy or pain ;
Endued with strong and resolute endurance
　　Till we shall take her to our hearts again.

But now, alas, with no such guerdon gifted,
　　And faith too often under deep eclipse,
The silence voiceless and the dark unlifted,
　　The cup so bitter pressing at our lips,

We move bewildered toward the heavenly city
　　To meet our Darling when the morn shall come.
Patience, O Father, grant ; O Jesus, pity !
　　Till Thy dear hand bring us to her and home.

## A PRAYER FOR LIGHT.

Through darkened days the sky hung low,—
The wind wailed mournfully, and slow
Went on the hours.   A wild storm poured
Its wrathful vials, fully stored
Upon the earth, until, dismayed,
Men, prayerless long, bowed down and prayed
For sight of heaven's fair face again,—
For the clear shining after rain.
And just at evening from the west
There shot a golden promise blest;
A rich and ruddy sunset ray—
A splendor of that perfect day
Which shines above the clouds alway—
One moment broke into our sight,
And died in swift-descending night.
But men who saw the parted sky,
The flash that gleamed so gloriously,
Smiled at the hopeful prophecy.
Is it not light O God, with Thee?

Casts e'er a rising cloud between
Thee and Thy works impervious screen?
I stand, I hope, I hold by this,—
With God all light, no darkness is.
    But over me the shadow bends;
On me the blinding storm descends;
'Tis darkness all.   My God, I cry,
Where is my hopeful prophecy?
Where shall I find the bright-edged rift
That lets light in?   O when shall lift
The chilling, cheerless, crushing pall
That wraps, obscures and stifles all?
    But change will come.   Trust is not vain;
There must be sunshine after rain;
After the darkness and distress
Must come the dawning day of peace.
Sweet voices tell me that so sure
As God is light enduring, pure,
Sometime from partings in the west
Shall come illumination blest.
Some gleam of God shall yet break through
To fire my struggling soul anew
With hope and courage.   I believe,

And yet 'tis dark.   Thou who did'st give
Thyself to be of men the light,
Shine through this envelope of night;
Guide Thou my darkened, troubled eye
Toward some window in the sky
Where I may see Thy blessed face,
And seeing, enter into peace.

O how her faithful hand we miss
From all the gentle ministries
    Of home and love;
Dear hand, laid down so still and cold,
The heavy mass of clay and mold
    Piled deep above.

As though she talked with One divine,
Love saw her face that it did shine;
    Now that is hid,
Dear face, beneath a mound of mold
And clay so dense and dark and cold,
    And coffin-lid.

Her heart so true in every beat,
So womanly and strong and sweet,
    We sadly laid,
Dear heart, so quiet, changed and cold,
Near other hearts hid in the mold,
    Of other dead.

And how from life her life we miss,
Her holy woman-ministries,
    None know but God ;
Dear life, of helpfulness untold,
Now quenched and lost beneath the cold
    Concealing sod.

## NATURE AND SORROW.

Appalled and desolate I stood,
  When my great sorrow fell,
Beneath a dense and rayless cloud;
  Amazed as in a spell.
My hope and very life were gone;
I faced that awful blank——ALONE!

It was so great and terrible,
  That giant grief of mine,
It seemed that earth and air might feel
  A sympathy divine;
That soulless things my hurt might see,
And give some sign they pitied me.

But day came up with joy and cheer;
  With light the world did flame;
And overhead their matins clear
  The birds sang just the same;
Just as in happy days they'd sung,
When all my joys and hopes were young;

When to my glad bewildered thought
   Nature rejoiced with me;
Bird-song and flowers and sunshine brought
   Their eager sympathy:
All knew and felt my joy it seemed;
Ah, simple child I was, who dreamed!

And when so swift and grievously
   My day of bruising came,
And midst the May-leaves over me
   The birds sang just the same,
And light and gladness in the air
Proclaimed that nature did not care,

It seemed to me a cruel wrong;
   For, foolish egotist,
I could not bear the gush of song,—
   The flowers by sunlight kissed.
"These gloried in my joy," I said;
"They mock me now beside my dead."

But if, in gladness or in tears,
   Love moves in my behoof,
Then is it best that nature wears
   This garment sorrow-proof,—

Best that there be no change, no sign
Of pain for anguish such as mine.

For when on human grief or bliss
   The sun pours cheerful flame,
When flowery petals dew-drops kiss,
   And birds sing just the same,
Do they not say, "Whate'er befall,
God's one great thought is love in all?"

They bid us lay our sore hearts down
   On the paternal breast
Of Him whose mighty thoughts move on
   The highway of the Best!
Whose gifts may bring the shroud and pall
But whose one thought is love in all.

## MARAH, ELIM, BOCHIM.

Up rose the race God purposed to deliver,
  With wives and children, in the night, in haste,
Threw off their servitude by Egypt's river,
  The blessings of their promised land to taste.

Then came swift flight and followed swift pursuing;
  Crying of women and despair of men ;
Hope of escape, foreboding of undoing ;
  The Red Sea passage and the triumph then.

Through dreary wilderness and desert places,
  Looking for palm-trees round perennial springs,
Homeless and worn, but with expecting faces,
  Journeyed the chosen of the King of kings.

Did not the Lord, His mighty presence lending,
  Go on before them in the cloud and flame ?
How blessed the journey, to what glorious ending !
  How glad beneath the shelter of His name !

So came they on to shade and water cooling,
    Through dust of desert and the glare ot sun,
Singing fit praise to Him who, overruling,
    Gave them refreshing·when the march was done.

But hark, a burst of loud and stormy wailing!
    Had Abraham's God enticed them with a lie?
Led them along till strong men's strength was failing,
    And then withdrawn to see them slowly die?

The place was Marah and the springs were bitter,
    And bitter speech came fast from lips of men ;
' Was this the promise to the fathers ? fitter
    The bondage with the food of Egypt then.'

And so the God who forth had called them led them
    To Marah now, and thence to Elims' palms ;
Taught them severely—smote them while he fed them,
    Gave storm and tempest after peaceful calms.

He gave them victory and great rejoicing,—
    The ringing timbrel and the dancing feet ;
He too gave Bochim with its plaintive voicing,
    With tears and shame and penitence replete.

So seems it still that whom He loves and chooses,
   Whom He inspires to seek a better land,
He leads by rugged desert paths, and uses
   The rod of chastening with a heavy hand.

He sends great pain to raptured joy succeeding,—
   First freedom's transport and then Marah's springs,
Elim and Bochim lie the way He's leading;
   The blessing and the bitterness He brings.

In some alembic, strange and secret blending,
   Sorrow and gladness one rich blessing grow;
To highest good not every joy is tending,—
   To deepest harm not every crushing woe.

And God gives both; we sing or weep before Him—
   Stand up exulting—bend like bruised reeds;
And ever for that clear-eyed faith implore Him
   To see the pillar or the flame that leads:

To know at Marah that our God is loving,
   Tenderly loving as at Elim blest;
Midst Bochim's tears to feel Him gently moving
   Our hearts toward Him for pure and trusting rest.

Do not I know?   What means the Lord?
'Tis not like Him, not like His word,
Who makes our countless troubles His,
And feels our oft infirmities !
He surely would not, could not say,
When sorrow drinks my life away—
When my best hope and joy and pride
Go down into the grave beside
The form so precious to my love—
In grief all other griefs above—
He would not say :   "Thou dost not know
The dark, mysterious thing I do."
Do not I know?   I, hurt and sore,
Yearning for joys that come no more,
For heart-communings and embrace,
For sound of voice and sight of face,
That, once to hear again and see,
Would fill my soul with ecstacy?
Is my whole nature dull and slow?

Can I not feel when falls a blow?
What means the Lord, "Thou dost not know?'
   I marked, for days, a summer-bird
Busy with hopeful cares; and heard
Her sing, as if entirely blessed,
Around the deep and crowded nest.
   But soon and swift a storm-burst came,
With wind and rain and lightning flame,
And crashing 'mid the swinging trees; '
And when it passed no vestiges
Of nest or tender young were found
On broken bough or littered ground.
   Did not she know, that parent bird,
Whose seeking, sorrowing note I heard,
That all her labor had been vain?
That blooming hope had fruit in pain?
   Writing upon the beaten sand
Of the sea's edge, with slender hand,
I saw a graceful girl.   A thing
Of idle, aimless dallying
It seemed; but anxious prophecies,
And hopes, and maiden's purposes
That filled her heart, but all unsaid,

On the hard sand were deftly spread.
Thus wrought she, all intent, alone;
Then long on what her hand had done,
She silent looked and mused and sighed.
  One forward wave from flowing tide
Came sliding up the smooth incline,
And dashed out every meaning sign.
  Did not she know that what her hand
Unconscious wrote on vacant sand
Had gone forever from her view,
As vanishes the early dew?
  So do I know what has been done;
From mid-day sky has dropped the sun;
My hope, appalled and tempest-tost,
Looks up no more, her anchor lost.
O, I *do* know; I feel and see   .
The heavy hurt that crushes me!
So, Lord, in pain, I answered Thee.
  I slept; and whiles, I knew not how,
The buds upon the apple-bough          .
Burst in each close and sharded fold,
And freed the leaves they had inrolled.
  I knew not how, but where the seed

Had fallen for the future's need,
I saw, on sharp and slender blade,
The hastening prophecy of bread.
   How wrought He these? I could not tell;
His ministers invisible
Had moved in light and dark and air,
—In secret working to prepare
The way before the living King—
The beauty, bloom, and hope of Spring.
His work I saw; but not the way
Each worker went.   The under-play
Of power was hid from sight like mine;
The work disclosed the hid design.
   So, if He say:   "Thou doest not know
The dark, mysterious thing I do,
But thou shalt know,"—I wait until
His unseen powers their task fulfill;
I wait, and, groping, pass through these
His strange and voiceless processes,
To learn with rapture at their end,
To what of good these bruisings tend.
I wait on Him who hides His thought
Sometimes, until the wonder wrought
Appears to our new-opening eyes,

God's love made clear, without disguise.
I wait, and bear the lingering smart
He knows is burning at my heart.
 .   I do believe Thee, Lord, and rest
On Thee my burden.   Sore oppressed,
Not knowing all Thou doest now,
Help me to wait my time to know ;
To wait until the blind shall see !
So, Lord, in faith, I answer Thee.

## NOT DEAD.

I think her living yet;
It cannot, ought not, must not be
That death hath conquered utterly;
That in the swift and fell surprise
That stilled her heart and sealed her eyes,
All died that we had loved and known,—
All died that knew and loved her own;
I think her living yet.

I think her living yet
Somewhere in God's infinity;
Somewhere, though hidden quite from me,
She being has—she walks in white,—
She knows the joy, she sees the light
Of those who reach the higher planes,
By secret ways of mortal pains;
I think her living yet.

I think her living yet
An angel bright, God's minister

All-beautiful, I think of her.
She so divinely formed to bless,
So rich in woman's tenderness,
God's hand might be to wipe a tear,—
His voice, with words of holy cheer.
    I think her living yet.

    I think her living yet.
Two little ones her mother-love
Asks for and finds and clasps above.
Their infant spirit-speech she hears,
And on her mother-heart she bears
Them fondly where the Shepherd leads,—
Where by still streams His flock He feeds.
    I think her living yet.

    I think her living yet.
In glad rejoicings round the Throne
She serves and sings—she, still my own,
Goes with the shining companies,—
The Great King in His beauty sees,—
A child gone home, she is not dead !
Her portion she's inherited.
    I think her living yet.

I think her living yet.
And when, in God's time, I pass on
To the good land where she has gone,
She'll meet me at the portal bright,—
She'll lead to Him who is the light
Of the King's city,—ever mine,
She'll walk with me the ways divine
  Where she is living yet.

## SONG IN THE NIGHT.

Night is here and veiling thickly
Mountain, valley, plain and river;
But its shade shall vanish quickly,—
Shafts of golden light shall quiver
   Soon along the eastern sky,
   Telling that the day is nigh.

Night is here, but not forever
Is dominion to it given;
Light must rule, but darkness never,—
So is pledged the might of Heaven.
   Light shall reign and darkness fly;
   Light shall haste to victory.

Night of evil, hateful, cruel,
Hence thy shadows shall be driven;
Never shalt thou have renewal,—
So is pledged the might of Heaven.
   Shines there now the prophet-ray,
   Eloquent of perfect day.

Night of sorrow, bitter, cheerless,
Soon thy terrors shall be lifted :
Faith looks through thee strong and fearless,
With the might of Heaven gifted ;
   Knowing that thy gloom shall fade,—
   Waiting, watching, not afraid.

Night of death thy morning cometh,—
Yes, to thee shall light be given ;
Jesus Christ thy fading doometh,—
He has pledged the might of Heaven.
   Day shall soon begin with Him,
   Without night or twilight dim.

# MISCELLANEOUS POEMS.

# MISCELLANEOUS POEMS.

## *IMMANUEL.*

*Read at the Christmas Festival of the Plymouth Church of Des Moines, Christmas Eve, 1872.*

Round resting flocks a shepherd guard
Through the still night kept watch and ward,
As, 'neath the sky in open field,
The shepherd-men from days of eld
Had kept their flocks.   No sign was seen
Foretelling change from what had been.
  As when from old Chaldaic Ur
Abraham came forth a wanderer,
The stars looked down with lambent flame;
All things continuing the same
As at the world's beginning.   Men
For what had long been looked again.

Still are the shepherds; round their camp
Stands the thick wall of midnight damp;
Still is the constellations' march
Along the firmamental arch;
All things are hid but heaven; as when
There comes to crushed, disheartened men,
Of dearest good and hopes bereft,
The thought that only God is left,—
So now, night hides from human eyes
All but the heavenly mysteries.
    Sudden there bursts a strange surprise,— .
Sudden, awe-struck, the shepherds rise,—
The deeps of heaven are open flung,—
Peals through the night an angel-song,—
Shine, through the dark, supernal fires
Flashing on robes of heavenly choirs,
Who, with the shout of God's good will,
Proclaim the Prince Immanuel.
    Celestial spirits joyful, thus
Announce His coming, God with us.
    To Bethlehem then, glad, wondering,
The shepherds go to hail a King.
They find no glittering, gorgeous train,—
For royal state they look in vain,—

They see no swift-built palace towers,
Nor throne nor pride of kingly powers;
But in a manger, lighted dim,
Where only earth has room for Him,
They see an infant child,—for thus
Came our Immanuel, God with us.

O holy, gracious infancy,
God ever comes to man in thee!
Comes near us in a little child,
Near us, with hands and hearts defiled,
To say, "Put off thy shoes, for round
An infant's couch is holy ground!"
Comes near, the heart's best life to stir
As by an angel messenger;
To teach us solemnly to say,
"God standeth near our souls to-day."
So does the Highest earthward turn,—
So into human households born,
He comes to us with advent sweet,
To turn to Him our wandering feet.

The Word made flesh, Immanuel came,
Still God with us in sin and shame,

Not with hard blows to smite us down,—
To blast us with indignant frown,—
But with dear pity to proclaim
That Love is the almighty name!
To show each sinning, fearful child
God's face, already reconciled;
As, penitent, we bow the knee,—
To say to each, "I pardon thee;
I ask not tears and long distress;
I, God's revealed forgivingness,
Bid thee arise and go in peace."


Our hopes take hold on glorious things,
Soaring with quick, ambitious wings;
They promise that we too shall rise,
Like God's great saints, to victories
O'er sins and oft infirmities.
We dare to hope that on the heights
Our feet shall walk, 'midst the delights
By valorous overcoming won,—
With those who blessed, obtaining, run.
Feet are not wings. We stumble, fall
As we go on. The weak and small

Affright, dismay and cast us down ;
Far off appears the victor's crown ;
And oft the foolish soul avers
That they who more than conquerors
Went on before, had grace from Heaven
Only to favored mortals given.
And so we pant and fear and sigh,
Know not the joy of victory,
And, full of shame and deep distrust,
Turn clouded faces toward the dust.
  To men o'erwhelmed, discouraged thus,
He comes, Immanuel, God with us,
Breaking no slender, bruised reed,
A patient, pitying friend indeed,
To say to each, "O downcast soul,
I am thy helper toward the goal.
Dost crave some shining victory ?
'Tis victory to walk with me
In valleys low and modest shade.
Take courage then—lift up thy head.
The saints who joyous highways trod
Could do no more than walk with God !
Thy heart, so troubled, rest on mine
And fear no more—God's strength is thine."

About us gathers mystery;
What is this *being*, and *to be?*
Offspring of God's creating power
Does He care for and love us more?
Is Father-hood reality?
Stoops it to find and succor me?

   Immanuel comes, a human form,
With all divinest passions warm;
Our human needs and pains and cares
He on his loving bosom bears.
No man so much a man as He,—
God perfecting humanity.

   O questioning heart and vision dim,
The Eternal Father see in Him,
Who from our weakness, sins and shames,
Exalts, delivers and redeems.


   Broken before the God we bless
We sink and suffer, comfortless.
A hurt is ours no heart can share,—
Which we can neither shun nor bear;
From deepest depths for help we cry;
Help in a life's extremity.

And He draws near and goes with us
Who wept o'er buried Lazarus:
He walks on gently by our side
Who for the love He bore us died:
No friend comes near us as does He,—
No heart so pours its sympathy.
To Him we turn from fear and dread;
In His dear love are comforted;
The bitterness He understands;
We feel the soothing of His hands;
In Him who seeks and helps us thus,
We see Immanuel, God with us.

Sing then to Him of Bethlehem!
Crown Him with love's pure diadem.
Ye children praise Him with the voice
Of childish gratitude —rejoice
In Him the manger held,—
In Him who God to man revealed.
All people praise Him,—all hearts sing
To Him God gave—a child—a King.
Give thanks aloud for God's good will
Proclaimed in our Immanuel.

## THE MOTHER'S SONG.

Nestling so gracefully,
Sleeping so peacefully
  My darling, my dove :
Dear Lord approvingly,
Tenderly, lovingly,
  Look from above.

Eyes that so merrily,
Pleasantly, cheerily,
  Sparkled and shone ;
Eyes that all tearfully,
Wonderingly, fearfully,
  Viewed the unknown.

Tongue that so wittily,
Saucily, prettily,
  Prattled at will—
Prattled untiringly,
Mother admiringly
  Listening still.

Mouth that appealingly,
Touchingly, feelingly,
  Trouble did tell;
Mouth which so speedily
Laughing right readily,
  Rang like a bell;

Lips where in cosiness,
Beauty and rosiness,
  Sweet kisses hide;
Lips where disdainfully,
Pettishly, painfully,
  Passion did bide;

Hands that all beautiful,
Teachable, dutiful,
  Fondled and played;
Hands that so skilfully,
Secretly, wilfully,
  Law disobeyed;

Feet that so lightsomely,
Trippingly, blithesomely,
  Sported and danced;

Feet whose sweet cheeriness
Wore into weariness
  As they advanced;

All nestling gracefully,
Slumbering peacefully
  Are ye to-night;
Quietly, trustfully,
Silently, restfully,
  Waiting for light.

O, best benefaction
And dearest attraction,
  Fairest that lives!
In sleep so beautiful,
All that's undutiful
  Mother forgives.

Now rest thee securely,
Sleeping so purely,
  My darling, my dove;
God's angels descending,
About thee attending,
  Keep thee in love.

## SYLVANUS OF MT. SINAI.

Time was when good men from all scenes defiled
Fled into caves and dens and deserts wild
To keep themselves from sin; gave up the fight
With Satan for the world; for God's dear right
To hold and rule the souls he made, gave o'er
The contest beaten; sadly fled before
Rough handed might and craft and lies and all
The infernal powers which held the world in thrall;
They fled from sin—they would themselves be pure;
They fled from vengeance hastening—at the door;
They saw the sign of near prophetic doom,
And sought for shelter from the wrath to come.
          Now in that fearful time of flight and haste,
When fittest covert was the wildest waste,
There came a band of Monks to Sinai.   Sin
Drove them out to fight in solitude.   In
That rugged wilderness of rock and earth
They hoped the new life might in them have birth
And grow.   Surrendering all they had, they came

To worship there the dear Christ's blessed name;
The outward man with toils and fasts subdue,
The inward man by prayer and faith renew.
        The good Sylvanus was their Abbot.   He,
Full both of wisdom and simplicity,
A worthy Father, ordered all their ways,
And pattern set in discipline and praise.
They worked to live; their simple wants supplied
By patient culture of the mountain-side.
The wilderness and solitary place
Gladdened around them with unwonted grace;
The rule held sway in that severe retreat,
"If none will work, then neither shall he eat."
With early morning, while the east was dim,
Up rose the incense of their matin hymn
And simple prayers.   Then forth they sped
To wrest from barrenness their daily bread.
        And while, one morn, they wrought beneath the sun
There came to them a priestly stranger: one
Who lived by faith, not works; a monk whose care
And glory were to keep himself by prayer.
Well kept he was, and saintly was his mien;
His rosary lay his unsoiled hands between.

Of salt sweat on his brow he liked no trace ;
But what by sweat of brow was won, with grace
And pious air in cool resort could eat,
Thanking the Lord who sends his servants meat.
      To them this stranger :
                " Know ye not who saith
Ye may not toil for meat that perisheth ?
I have that gospel written in my heart ;
I follow Mary choosing the good part ! "
      Sylvanus meekly said :
                "Thou choosest well.
Go, Brother Paulus, show this monk a cell
And book.   Give him naught more."
            Their task went on ;
The sun rose higher, neared his going down.
The monks of Sinai rested from the strain
Of work, ate their plain fare, then wrought again
Until the vesper hour was nigh.   None said,
"Where's the strange brother?  Should he not be fed ?"
All left him to the Abbot.
            In the cell
The monk constrained himself to read ; then fell
Upon his face and prayed ; his sins confessed ;

Penance revolved and smote upon his breast ;
Then read again the book ; his soul alert
To give no vantage to the mass inert
Of his vile body, despicable, base,
Of countless sins the nurse and hiding place.
But as time flew his thoughts likewise took wing
And wandered widely ; a forbidden thing.
He thought of food : reproved himself and prayed.
"A noble fashion have these monks," he said.
"They mortify the flesh ; fast sin away ;
Shall I not equal them ?   Oh, let me pray."

      He fought a losing fight.   His fleshly foes
To greater insolence each hour arose.
The carnal trampled the superior soul ;
The body urgent clamored for control.
The book, the prayer, the penance lost the power
To hold his mind to duty.   Every hour
Spirit grew faint and feeble, flesh grew strong ;
Devotion vanished as the day waxed long.
      And in despair he cried :
                "Shall these men win
Their crowns by such heroic discipline,
And I lose mine?   They work and fast ; while I

Pray the day long, but gain not mastery.
These Sinai monks seem made of sternest stuff;
Their discipline is like their mountain, rough!"
  The monk was hungry, and his hunger made
His cell a cage, his prayers pretense: it played
With carnal thoughts of more than Lenten fare—
A Devil's tempter to the man of prayer.
  At length he yielded; sought the Abbot; said;
"Do not you ask the Lord for *daily* bread?
Do not you eat it daily when 'tis given,
And, eating, bless the generous grace of Heaven?
Do not the brethren eat at all to-day?"
  "Yes," said the Abbot.
        "Why not call me, pray?"
And then Sylvanus said:
        "Thou dost not need,
As others do, on fruits and bread to feed.
*We* all are carnal.  We must eat because
We work.  To earth this earthy nature draws.
But thou, so blessed with faith, so rich in heart,
Need'st not to eat!  Thou'st chosen the good part."
  Whereat the stranger was ashamed, 'tis said,
That he should only pray, not work, for bread.

## JOHN OF MT. SINAI.

Among the Sinai monks the brother John,
A shrunk and dwarfish man, was numbered; one
Who winced beneath the burden of the cross;
And while he claimed to count his gain but loss
For Christ, he counted grudgingly the gain
He lost, and gave it up for Christ with pain.

And when to labors till the evening damp
Were added vigils by the midnight lamp,
Abundant hardships after meager fare,
Of sleep o'er little, and o'er much of prayer,
The monk's vocation seemed no easy yoke
And burden light, of which the Master spoke.
He bore it with impatience.   Poor, unwise,
He dwelt upon the pain of sacrifice
And lost its blessing.   In his troubled breast
His wrung soul cried a bitter cry for rest.

"Behold," said he, "the lilies, how they grow!
They toil not, spin not, yet I surely know

They give God glory which He pleased receives,
And them His easy service never grieves.

"The angels, too, in their celestial spheres,
No flagellations have, nor fasts, nor tears
To make their service bitter.    Only men
Serve God with utter wretchedness."    And then
He vowed to break the chains the brothers wore,
And run their toilsome treadmill round no more ;
To give himself away to God, and free
His soul from care.    As angels live, so he
Would live thereafter—by God's grace sustained,—
The world become his paradise regained.

He turned from Sinai and the monks away,
Threw off as needless his rough cloak of gray,
(For Angel life could ask no mortal gear)—
And sought, far off, the Presence ever near.

Into the desert waste, the solitude
Which girt the mountain round, where scanty food
Or drink or cooling shade existed, went
The eager man, to rest with God intent.
To be as the white angels are, his prayer ;

To walk with them—their easy service share.
  So seven days went by.  The brotherhood
Surprised, amazed at John's exalted mood,
Spoke little of the wanderer; and when
They mentioned him, those simple monkish men
Devoutly crossed themselves on breast and brow
And said, " Our brother's with the angels now!
He rose up with a simple, daring faith
And cast himself on God, not waiting death."

  But those few days sore trial brought to John,
Shelterless, friendless, in the desert lone.
From the forgetful heaven no manna fell.
No spring leaped out of rock.  No visible
Appearance proved that God took kindly note
Of his pressed servant.  From fat lands remote
No raven came his daily bread to bring.
In their strong arms no angels ministering
Bore up the wanderer lest his weary feet
Against the sharp, injurious stones should beat.
The sun smote him by day.  By night the wind
Shriveled and pierced him with its blasts unkind .
The desert scared him with its aspect rude;

Not that way lay the path to angelhood
And beatific joys.   The monk a man
Remained—a mortal pinched, forlorn and wan.
He could not cast himself on God.   In vain
With tears he strove desired release to gain
From the sore burden that his life had been ;
From toil and care and cross as well as sin.

And as the seventh day went darkly down,
And all his brother monks were housed, poor John
Came stumbling in the night, seeking the door
He left with highest hope one week before.
He knocked.   The Abbot heard within and cried,
" Who knocks?"  " 'Tis I, 'tis John," a voice replied.
"Nay," said the Abbot,  " John no more with men
Hath part or lot.   He comes not here again
From his high company.   With shining throngs
Of angels now he walks—to them belongs."

The door was shut.   Nor earth nor man had place,
Angels nor God, for one who had not grace
To serve the Lord with patience.   Down John fell
Along the threshold weeping.   The strong swell

Of his sore spirit shook him.   Long he cried
For the forgiveness of the crucified,
The suffering Christ who, patient, bore the cross
That men for Him might count all gain but loss.
    And then the angels came to John; while he
Essayed no more as angels are to be,
Nor sought them, lo, they came to him; and peace
New-found, poured through his soul its blessedness.

    And in the morning, when the door stood wide,
John took his place close at the Abbot's side,
And said, "Forgive me that I went astray.
Forget my foolish weakness.   As I lay
Last night without, the pitying Master came ;
He spoke me tenderly, called me by name,
And said to me, 'Serve me content as man.
For man, not angel, was the Gospel plan.
Give me a patient human love.   Obey
My rule ; for my sake bear the cross ; then may
The angels see and wonder at above
The beauty of a soul renewed by love.' "

    And thenceforth John, until the day he died,

Served in his place with patience ; mortified
The flesh, and as a true, repentant man,
Gave Christ the service that no angel can.

## THE RIVER TO THE NIGHT.*

O welcome, yes welcome, thou blessed night!
   Thrice welcome art thou to me;
In thee I may go with a peaceable flow
     Far on to the measureless sea,—
     The sea that is waiting for me.

O cruel and galling the yoke I wear;
   Dark night I murmur to thee;
In bondage I go with laborious flow
     To rest in the welcoming sea,—
     The sea that is calling to me.

O freedom, dear freedom, no longer mine,
   My thoughts are ever of thee:
Ne'er again shall I know the rapturous flow

---

* This piece was composed while the writer was residing in the valley
of one of those hard-worked New England rivers, of which so much is
exacted on the way to the ocean.

That once marked my way to the sea,—
The sea that was asking for me.

O music, sweet music, merciful night,
    Is thy deep silence to me ;
A story of woe is my turbulent flow
      Down, down to the sheltering sea,—
      The sea that is refuge for me.

The story is long of my bondage to wrong ;
I cannot portray the half in my song.
Far, far to the north into light I leaped forth
As free as the bird to sing through the earth ;
To the hills with my voice I shouted, "Rejoice!"
And echo caught up the jubilant noise,
And the hail of the rill to each answering hill
Repeated, in shouts that never were still.
The trees, as in love, waved their banners above,
And laughed as I kissed the feet of the grove ;
Over me in my bed their branches they spread,
A shield from the sun that blazed overhead.
I gathered the brooks from inviolate nooks
Of mountain recess and sentinel rocks,
To journey with me as unbridled and free,

A child of delight, I rolled to the sea.
The grasses that grew on my either bank drew
Their life from my depths, their delicate hue.
The birds dipped the bill, quickly drinking their fill,
And rendered their thanks with warble and trill.
I bore the lillies sweet-scented flotillas,
Wafting afar to hamlets and villas                    .
Breath sweetly laden for lover and maiden,—
Incense like that of morning in Eden.
I mirrored the grace and the sportive embrace
Of children, down-looking into my face.
My will I obeyed as I loitered in shade,
Still lying and dark in thicket and glade,
Creeping through sedges, mad darting down ledges:
Swirling I dashed midst boulders and wedges
Of rough, riven rock, as, with laughter and mock,
I burst away aught my progress would block.
No hard master ruled me—glad, triumphing, free,
I joyfully journeyed on to the sea.

　　　But alas for the days, alas for the ways
I sadly recall—regretfully praise.
My freedom is gone—now a master I own,

And wearing his yoke I murmur and moan.
I grind in the mill; I am broke on the wheel;
I beat out my life on copper and steel;
The oak, mountain giant, gnarled, defiant,
I cut and shape to all uses pliant.
The spindles I drive and the looms, in that hive
Where man and machine seem both all alive.
From dawn's early gray till the light fades away,
Like Samson, I in the prison-house play.
Afar I am led from my own chosen bed;
Am beaten to foam—to tatters am shred.
Once all the day long the bright birds blent their song
In chorus above as I stole along;
Now I scarcely can hear their melodies clear,
So loud whir the wheels and rattle their gear;
And I painfully go, bruised, broken and slow,
To rest after toil in the ocean below.


Then welcome, yes welcome thou blessed night,
  The rest thou bringest to me;
In darkness I know brief repose as I go
    On, on to my home in the sea,—
    The sea that is thirsting for me.

A vision, stern vision, thou tyrant man,
  Of fate that hangs over thee :
Time's river doth go, with hurrying flow,
  On, on to the infinite sea,—
  The sea that is waiting for thee.

## DREAM-LAND.

When the mind is worn and weary,
With the strain of thought oppressed,
When the body spent with toiling
Languishes for quiet rest,
Grateful is the glowing setting
Of the sun behind the west.
Welcome are the sunset shadows,
Lengthened by the level beams
Till the child looms up a giant,—
Till the mound a mountain seems.
Welcome is the solemn darkness,—
So each weary laborer deems,
As he floats on sleep's soft pinions
Toward the mystic land of dreams.
Once within the enchanted border,
Enters he another life
Strangely colored and fantastic,
With a new experience rife ;

He, no unconcerned spectator
Of its scenes of joy or strife.
Wandering forth from sleep's still prison
While the body silent lies,
Close before his crowded vision
Forms of beauty thronging rise,
And he, earnest, gazes on them
With his ravishrd spirit-eyes.
Gladly too, he goes among them,
With a bright and kindly band
Of the dream-folk, who stand ready,
Taking his freed spirit-hand,
To conduct him midst the wonders
Of their wonder-teeming land;
Of the land where no conception
So unreal is or wild
That it may not be embodied;
Where existence is beguiled
By a fairer ministration
Than on waking man has smiled;
Where for each disturbing sorrow
Flows the soft Lethean spring,
And the hurt heart, for the moment

Feels no touch of suffering;
Where no forms of coming evil
Their ill-omened shadows fling.
There our cherished air-built castles
From their shapeless ruins rise,
Standing sure, though unsupported,
Till they touch the vaulted skies,
And we see each rising wonder
Without question or surprise.
  Now these flitting dream-land spirits
Memory's treasures open throw,
And her dearest, costliest riches
Gilt with dream-land sunlight glow.
Now they summon our companions,—
Cherished friends of long ago,
Scattered earth-wide,—gone forever,—
Gone on that returnless flow
Of the life-stream, going, going
Fast, but whither none may know.
These come back to glad re-unions,—
Come their love for us to show;
Come with all their charm and beauty,
Losing no remembered grace,

Lay their sweet touch on our forehead,
Lay upon our own their face,
Speak the deep things of the spirit,
And the lost so long replace.
  Or these dream-folk act the prophet
Of a joy that soon shall be,
Light the coming days with promise,
Bid us lift our eyes and see
That the best things we have hoped for
Have become reality;
That they bring the treasured future
With each good it has in store
Backward to the living present,—
With the joy which lies before
Mingling that already tasted,—
Joy, when waking, known no more.
  Very beautiful is dream-land
With its gladsome forms of light;
Clouds need there no silver lining,
For they are as silver bright;
But I think of the awaking,
When all dreams shall take their flight,
And I ask "what now is coming?"

With a hush akin to fright,
For I see these glib-tongued prophets
Seldom prophesy aright.

www.ingramcontent.com/pod-product-compliance
Lightning Source LLC
Chambersburg PA
CBHW022021080426
42733CB00007B/677